52 POEMS *for* 52 WEEKS
A Lunar Year

First published 2020 by Gifted Muslim Ltd.
www.giftedmuslim.com
mail@giftedmuslim.com

British Library Catalogue in Publication Data:
a catalogue record for this book is available from the British Library
ISBN 978-1-9160465-4-2

52 POEMS FOR 52 WEEKS
A LUNAR YEAR

A collection of poems organised into the twelve Islamic Months

Yes, you're correct. There aren't 52 weeks in the lunar calendar.
It's just that 52 sounds better than 51, right?

Written by
Abdullah Mansoor

Contents

Jumada Al-Awwal

Jumada Al-Thani

Rajab

Sha'ban

Ramadan

Shawwal

Dhul Qa'dah

Dhul Hijjah

Congratulations to my children for contributing two poems to this collection. Dawood and Haneef, may the Most Wise bless you and increase you in beneficial knowledge.

Introduction

In front of you, you have a collection of poems written in different styles. I have attempted to create meaningful, flowing and, at times, light-hearted poems that will reach out to each individual that breathes in the words expressed for enjoyment, enlightenment and reflection.

You will find various different styles that have been adopted, namely: sonnet; ballad; haiku; limerick; acrostic and free verse. Each poem follows a particular metre and rhyming pattern. Further explanation of this can be found later in this book.

The Structure

As the title suggests, the poems have been arranged into each month of the Islamic calendar.

There are four poems for each month, except for Ramadan, where there are seven. While many months contain a poem, or poems, that may reflect within it a sense of belonging for that particular month, this is not always the case.

To aid the flow of reading, each poem has been presented without any background information. However, should you wish to gain some insight into the backgrounds of certain poems, you will find this immediately after the final poem. This will include the meanings of Arabic words used as well as any other useful details.

To end on a high note, you will be pleased to find a section for you to explore your poetry writing skills with the help of templates and some prompts.

The information presented after the background section may also be useful when reading the poems in the book, as well as when attempting to write your silky smooth poems.

I sincerely hope that you enjoy the poems that have been written to express the chaos in my mind as well as shed some light on this beautiful faith that I hold dearly.

Abdullah Mansoor

ISLAMIC MONTHS

"Indeed, the number of months with Allah is
twelve [lunar] months in the register of Allah"
[Quran, 9:36]

رَبِيع الثَّاني Rabi' Al-Thani	رَبِيع الأَوَّل Rabi' Al-Awwal	صَفَر Safar	مُحَرَّم Muharram
شَعبَان Sha'ban	رَجَب Rajab	جُمَادَى الثَّاني Jumada Al-Thani	جُمَادَى الأَوَّل Jumada Al-Awwal
ذُو الحِجَّة Dhul Hijjah	ذُو القَعدَة Dhul Qa'dah	شَوَّال Shawwal	رَمَضَان Ramadan

Muharram

The Provision

We start the day with *bismillah*,
Adventures near and far
Will need the blessings of Allah
On foot or in a car.

The birds they fly and come back full
From morning till sky bleeds,
No need to scurry chasing wind
One always meets one's needs.

But don't sit thinking *rizq* is near
Go out and try to earn,
Allah's decree we shouldn't fear
To Him we shall return.

A Great Occasion

A great occasion we can see
When Musa led the people free
From sweat, abuse and abjectness
Of Pharaoh and his viciousness
Towards a promise from their Lord
A life of peace again restored.

The signs that Allah gave to them
Were plenty and He gave again,
From locusts, blood and then a plea
They saw the splitting of the sea,
And so the Children of Israel
Were free as evil Pharaoh fell.

#3

Sonnet of Faith

Allah decrees and all there is will be.
His angels made of light, so bright and pure,
Their status high, they glorify and see
His plan for man – to send Jibreel with cure.

The scriptures sent to guide humanity
To treat the greed and all that He abhors,
The prophets strove against great tyranny
They led the way to mercy and much more.

Reminding masses of the Final Day,
A day when none shall side with whom they bore,
And all that was decreed shall come to weigh
The good and bad of destiny assured.

This is the faith I love with all my heart;
I pray to Him to never let me part.

4

A Pure Love: Love of the Prophet Muhammad (ﷺ)

My heart is yearning for your love
   although I feel unsure
I wonder how, oh if at all,
   a love can be so pure.

I search the nights devoid of light
   for He's the One Who knows
The servant's plea for His decree
   to dry the tear that flows.

Your loss to me shall never be
   surpassed by anyone,
Each time I feel a loss so deep
   Your loss is matched by none.

My dear beloved, chosen one,
   it's you I long to see
Beside the pond of *Al-Kauthar*
   From you I shall not flee.

Safar

All By Allah's Permission

Renowned for its atrocities
But life has much adversities.

No evil we attribute to
This month we shall be going through.

The trials and tests we all must face
Can raise us high or cause disgrace,

So any act that one commits
Is only what Allah permits.

The way we plan and act upon
The year ahead will carry on.

We keep with us what we require
Intentions and a clear desire.

Sojourn

The year is in its infancy,
A baby cries for milk you see
For love and warmth are all we need
To be the best that we can be.

As we embark on this sojourn
Remembering the twists and turns,
The people that have helped us on
Won't be with us when we return.

The end is not so far away,
With evil friends we shall not stay
The day when everyone will flee
With actions shown without delay.

So let me be the one to say
The reason why my hair is grey
Is thinking of the time to come
When I'll be right or gone astray.

The Purple Sky

I see the purple sky above
    The moon a glowing light,
A cry from baby wakes up mum
    A gentle hush goodnight.

I see a famished cat behind
    a box - waiting to prowl
As little mice run on the streets
    I hear a red fox growl.

I see my neighbour's lights turn on
    as other people sleep,
The second hand tick-tocks away
    Then my alarm goes beep.

I see myself in changing gowns
    A warmth before I pray,
The night is when Allah is near
    My heart softens from clay.

A Gentle Whistle

A gentle whistle of the wind
Does graze the souls of those who've sinned,
And those who've sinned look on and stare
Admiring folk as they compare
A life that led them to this path,
A path so twisted, full of wrath.

They'd rather be with holy ones,
The ones that even saytan shuns.

But do these sinless souls exist?
From evil deeds do they resist?
How do they manage to comply?
Or do they live above the sky?
Perhaps, that's it! They cannot err
To err is human – feelings stir.

Rejoice the sinner grazed by wind
The Lord forgives those who have sinned.

Rabi' Al-Awwal

Return to Life

The footsteps in the frosty grass
    They start to melt away,
The cycles in the old garage
    The kids begin to play.

The birds that flew to warmer air
    They start to come back home,
The pear tree near the garden fence
    Sees bees come round to roam.

As everything returns to life
    The sun begins to shine,
I thank Allah for all He gives
    This pleasant life of mine.

Ifs and Buts

Child:
> If I were a lion, I'd roar loudly
> I'd show them who's boss and do it proudly!

Mum:
> But you're not a fierce lion, so
> this is how the poem should go...

Child:
> If I were a bird, I'd fly all day
> Up and down through the clouds I'd play!

Mum:
> But you're not a gliding bird, so
> this is how the poem should go...

Child:
> If I were a whale, king of the sea
> I'd make sure everyone listens to me!

Mum:
> But you're not a big strong whale, so
> this is how the poem should go...

I'm a little soul, fierce and proud
I sleep all night and wake up loud,
I swing up high into the sky
My feet stretched out like I can fly,
I dive real deep into my pool,
I'm the swimming king – I'm so cool!

The Leaf

Leaf hangs on barely —
Gush of wind flings it around,
Settles down calmly.

The Worm

The pigeon flew down to the ground,
The little worm heard the sound;
It raised its head
Looked round and said
'Hey, look what I've just found!'

Rabi' Al-Thani

Assalaamu 'alaikum Dad

Assalaamu 'alaikum Dad,

I'm writing this message because I feel sad
I had to leave my friends and I wasn't glad.
Just as I was getting to know them better
I guess I'll have to write them a long letter
Telling them how gloomy I feel
The friendship we built felt so real.
But now I'm alone starting again
In a brand new school as I turn ten.

Wassalaamu 'alaikum

Assalaamu 'alaikum daddy dear,

I'm writing this message so you don't fear
I think you'll like what you're about to hear.
The lessons are fun and teachers cool
I've made new friends at my brand new school.

I'm learning new things every day
Just last week I learnt how to pray.
So thank you dad for sending me
To this new school where I'm happy.

Wassalaamu 'alaikum,

Haneef

By Haneef Abdullah

#14

Meant to Be

The soul knows what it knows
The tree grows when it grows
The universe is in peace
But us humans...

Conversations at the Zoo

A friendly lion came to me,
He raised his chin and said
'How wonderful to see you dear
Now, could you itch my head?'

A cheery parrot flew to me
And opened up her beak
'You seem like you're a lovely child
If only you could speak.'

A hungry hippo strolled to me
And with a mighty yawn
'Do you have anything to eat?
My breakfast is all gone.'

A cheeky monkey jumped to me
And scratched his hairy head
'Are you the one who pleases us
Or do we please you instead?'

Breakdown in Communication

'Woof woof' said the dog.
'Meow meow' said the cat.
'What?' said the rat.
And that was the end of that.

Jumada Al-Awwal

A Journey Home

I enter all alone this home
 Not knowing where to go,
I pass the room where Freedom lives
 Good friend from long ago.

Along the corridor I move
 By chance I meet Respect
And Honour staying right next door
 Close by as I'd expect.

I wonder if there's anymore
 Of friends that I adore,
I find Peace praying on the mat
 A breeze blows through the door.

This place I've come to call my home
 Its furniture is dreams,
I am the one who's known as Love
 Together we're a team.

This life is just a journey home,
 Once lost but we shall be
Together with our loved ones soon
 Together we'll be free.

The Poem That Explains the Main Reason Why Prophet Muhammad (ﷺ) Was Sent to All of Humanity

You were sent
as a mercy
to the whole world.

#19

Not All Glum

In the days to come
I'll look back and realise
It wasn't all glum.

#20

The Procrastinator

Do it tomorrow.
Should have done it yesterday.
There's still so much time...

Jumada Al-Thani

Brother and Sister

Brother and sister
Fight fight fight!
Starts in the day
Lasts through the night.

Brother and sister
Fight fight fight!
'He took my toy!'
'She pinched my bike!'

Brother and sister
Fight fight fight!
'She broke my chair!'
'He pulled my hair!'

Brother and sister,
Fight fight fight!
'He ate my cake!'
'She called me snake!'

But when trouble comes
From another
Brother and sister
Are there for each other.

#22

Dear Son

Dear son,

I hope this reaches you in time,
In time so you can see the route
Of those who tread the righteous line;
This message is not absolute.

My son, with Allah don't ascribe
A partner, He is the Most High,
To do so would be a great crime
Your soul would fall and want to cry.

My son, take heed of what I say,
Respect your parents after Him
Your mother bore you - now she's grey,
Don't ever let your light go dim.

My son, avoid the wrong you see
For something wrong cannot be right,
As small as mustard seed may be
Your Lord will bring it out to sight.

My son, stay firm on your salah
And call the people to what's right,
Remind to keep the wrong afar
Be patient as the calm of night.

Do not belittle those around,
Remember we're all from one man
So speak to people with soft sound
And walk this route the best you can.

#23

Eating Flesh

But it's all true what I've just said
Her lips are small, her eyes are red
And when I squint my eyes I see
A spot so big it frightens me!

What about him, soft as jelly?
He likes to fill his big round belly!
Yesterday I ate with him
I swear, he needs to join the gym.

I only speak about what's true
It's not like meat that I can't chew
And if they walk in past that crowd
I'll just deny and laugh out loud.

They'll take my deeds I hear you say
I have enough, I think, anyway.

Our Friends

We are our friends
And our friends are us
We sit together
We laugh together
We cry together
Together we are us

We are our friends
And our friends are us
I go next to them
And I smell of musk

We are our friends
And our friends are us
I go next to them
And return with dust

I choose my friends
And I choose to be us
I choose my friends
The good among us

Rajab

The Countdown

This is the month we start to seek
The blessings found therein
With hope of reaching Ramadan
Forgiveness for our sins

O Allah bless us in this month
The month that follows too
And let us reach the month you chose
The one after these two

The Night Journey

This sacred month is due respect
  A month that gives us peace,
No fighting nor creating harm
  All people live with ease.

This is the month where *al-ameen*
  Was taken from Makkah,
He mounted on the fast *buraq*
  And landed in *Aqsa*,

From there the honour of *miraj*
  Was granted to *al-'abd*,
The wonders of the creation
  Was shown from up above.

He reached the end where none had passed
  His status was so high,
Allah allowed him to proceed
  To which he did comply.

That night was when the Almighty
    Had gifted Muhammad (s)
The prayers you and I hold dear
    To which we're devoted.

And by the end of his journey
    The Prophet saw so much,
When he returned to go to sleep
    His bed was warm to touch.

My Dad

I wonder if my dad
Feels scared or even sad.

When I see spiders in my room
My dad removes them with a broom.

When I feel frightened in the night
My dad comes in and it's all right.

When we go flying in a plane
With his soft touch I'm calm again.

When I fall down and hurt my knee
He sits me down beside the tree.

In Ramadan his cry I hear –
Is this my dad that has no fear?

I understand why dad's so bold
I'll be right with him when he's old.

Me

I'm feeling so lonely
With people around me
They don't understand me
I think they can't hear me.

I'm screaming inside me
From thoughts that will haunt me
But nobody sees me
I should just let it be.

With no one to help me
How can I be set free?
This prison that holds me
Is killing me slowly.

I need to keep calling
So someone can show me
A light that will lead me
Away from the trapped me.

Sha'ban

Nearly There

The month that's number eight
 Brings blessings to the one
Who gives in charity
 And all that can be done.

The Prophet fasted in
 The blessed month Shaban,
One other month was more
 And that was Ramadan.

O Lord help us to reach
 The month when it arrives,
For no one can be sure
 If they will be alive.

Averter of Calamity

They say that charity will help
　　The giver of her wealth
And even if there's nothing left
　　At least she has her health.

If charity can help her shield
　　From trials and poverty
Indeed it's worth remembering
　　To give abundantly.

Supporting orphans is so great
　　A chance for her to be
Together with the best of men,
　　The Prophet's company.

But when she has no wealth to give
　　No money for a while
She looks around at things to gift
　　Her face can give a smile.

Removing objects from the street
   Is also charity
To stop and help a needy one
   Can help with clarity.

So when she's down and has no one
   Increasing charity,
As long as it's for Allah's sake,
   Averts calamity.

Shopping List

I have a shopping list
And nothing should be missed:

- Extra days of fasting (measure in *hasanat*)
- Bags full of charity
- Containers to give help to others
- A bottle to control anger
- A clock to pray on time
- Fresh *mushaf* of the Quran

Oh, and some dates for your Gran.

I See You

I see you standing still
With messy hair
And a face bare

      I see your smile upside down
      A tear in your eye
      A lonely sigh

            I see hope that's escaped
            A bruise near your cheek
            And cuts on your feet

      I see a love that's lost
      Dirt on fingertips
      And cracks on your lips

   I see your imperfections
   as I stand facing you
   And when you turn away
   I don't see you

I don't see you
But I feel you
Your grief is mine
And I'll be here for you

Ramadan

The Beloved Guest

Revered you are - you are the guest we love
to greet and hold on days and nights we plead
to Him who sent, Who knows what we all need,
You bring with you desire to please above
our *nafs*, in this we shall embrace true love,
What can be said of how you make us feel?
To us your light and peace are so surreal;
Rejoice the sight of light so white as doves.

Alas! We know this love shall not remain
As thirty days conclude we start to feel
your grace depart accompanied with pain,
Our Lord – Who sent our guest to help us heal –
let not our deeds and tears wind up in vain,
Help us stay strong, when guest is gone, with zeal.

Ask the One

Let the one who drowns in sorrow
Ask the One who brings the morrow

Feeling anguish causes torment
Asking Him will ease the moment

How can one despair so quickly
Knowing none can match His mercy

Thankful servant in the evening
Loving Master always giving

O the One Who answers timely
Make this night not end abruptly

The 25th Night

Striking is the sense of life on the 25th night.

Will the rebellious man stand
    or will he feel fright?
Will the heedless woman cry
    while this moon is still white?
Will the haughty child sit
    or will he take flight?
Will the couple make peace
    or will they still fight?

Perhaps it's time to sit, reflect and recite...

O Allah, you are most forgiving and you love
forgiveness, so forgive me tonight.

27th Night: A Sonnet for the Lonely

Detest the one that makes me feel alone,
Today I went to find myself a friend;
His door was shut, for this my heart bemoans.
Is this the month I thought my soul would mend?

The *masjid* closed, my home feels cold – I grieve,
My mum and dad are all I have – no more!
I left the ones I love, was I naive?
Is this the faith I chose, is this the cure?

For years I searched the days and nights for You,
You are the One Who guides my heart aright;
This is the month rewards I shall accrue,
My loneliness will fade away tonight.

Adore the One that makes me feel alive!
You love, forgive – for You I shall survive.

28th Night: Reminisce

As the end draws near
We reflect and reminisce
Of the days gone by.

29th Night: Fortunate Ones

It's come, it's here, the final one
   We have one night to find
the light that's sent by Lord of all,
   Forgiveness not declined.

How wrong were we to think about
   the lavish spread we craved,
The stomach churned from hunger, though
   desires were oft enslaved.

O Merciful is He the One
   Who loves that we repent,
Our sins and wrongs He shall replace
   with deeds without a dent.

The month of mercy leaves us now
   but He will always be
Rahman, *Raheem* to all His slaves,
   How fortunate are we.

30th Night: The Last Slice

A child grabs the cake –
gobble! There's only one piece.
Savour its delight.

Shawwal

Eid Poem

Enter the first day of Shawwal
Into the blessed day of Eid
Do *takbeer*, eat some dates and off to the *masjid*

Munch into my lovely brunch
Unwrap my special gifts
Before my brother gets to them
Alhamdulillah we share our toys
Ready to visit relatives
After a day of excitement and joy
Keeping these memories in my heart to cherish

By Dawood Abdullah

I'm Good Enough

I drew a bird with spread out wings
    Kate drew white clouds of fluff
The teacher gave the clouds high praise
    Was I not good enough?

I sang in front of the whole school
    And Dave gave out a huff
The teacher clapped loud for his part
    Was I not good enough?

I studied hard to get top grades
    They said this year was tough
But Linda was accepted on
    Was I not good enough?

At work I was the one who found
    solutions to stern stuff
But Barry was promoted up
    Was I not good enough?

I walked my children to the park
    That's when I saw the cuffs
Disgraced in front of everyone
    Was I not good enough?

I prayed to God to give me strength
    Those times had been so tough
Would He ignore the one who calls
    Would I be good enough?

The One Who watches from His Throne
    Is never unaware
He answers those who call on Him
    And saves us from despair.

Irrelevant is how we look
    A diamond starts out rough
To please the One Who grants success
    I know I'm good enough.

#42

Eid Cake

There once was a boy who liked cake,
For Eid he wanted to bake;
But mummy was busy
So he accidentally
Put inside it a snake.

The One

Say He is Allah the Only One
Our Lord the Master of the Throne

He is Eternal, Self Sufficient
We ask of Him as we're deficient

He's not a father or a son
As He created everyone

To Him we make no equal partner
Akin to Him there is no other.

Dhul Qa'dah

The Call

I call on you to hear a sound that's best

Allah is the greatest
Allah is the greatest

He is the one I worship, I declare
His messenger is Muhammad, that I swear

A call to prayer that's good for you
A call to success in all you do

Allah is the greatest
Allah is the greatest

He is the one I worship, I declare

So come my friend before it's late
Come join in and embrace your fate

#45

Dad, Sam and Jack the Donkey

They took a donkey into town
    For business dad had there,
As Sam sat on the back of Jack
    A man shouted "unfair!"

Now dad sat on the donkey's back
    A woman this time claimed
"A dad like this deserves a smack"
    So dad stepped down ashamed,

And with great thought they forged a plan
    They both sat on the brute
But soon enough they heard a man
    "You both deserve the boot!"

The pair not knowing how to go
    Decided on their track
To show the crowd their virtue, so
    propped donkey on their backs.

The people now could not believe
    They mocked both son and dad,
It seems that people will perceive
    What they think good and bad.

#46

The Magpie

I tried to help a magpie fly
    Her injured wings were clipped,
She couldn't find her way up high
    Instead she jumped and skipped.

She couldn't ask for any help
    Her parents lost to her,
No screaming, shouting or a yelp
    Things must've been a blur.

I gave her water to consume
    Her beak was pecking fast,
I prayed her life would soon resume
    Before she breathed her last.

Before too long she gained her might
    And spread her mended wings,
The magpie flew to my delight
    Her voice an echoed ring.

Weekly Plan

<u>Monday</u>
Is when my iron duvet
Won't let me get out of bed

<u>Tuesday</u>
Is when my lights turn on
To view the week ahead

<u>Wednesday</u>
Is a productive day
I'm like a buzzing bee

<u>Thursday</u>
Is for winding down
Looking forward with glee

<u>Friday</u>
Is the fudge cake of all days
A mini Eid if I can say

<u>Saturday</u>
Is full of fun
Rest, laughter and play

<u>Sunday</u>
Is the end of the chapter
Looking to my iron duvet

Dhul Hijjah

#48

A Flashback

The days of Hajj are nearing us,
   A flashback of the time
I went to see the holy place
   Atoning for my crime,
I wasn't sure what I would feel
   This mountain I would climb.

The people and the history
   As I fulfilled the rites,
Had helped me gain a sense of joy
   Which helped me reach great heights,
I came away with all my deeds
   In front of my Lord's sight.

The journey of a lifetime gave
   My heart serenity;
If I were to return again
   At home my soul would be.

I Really Want to Go

I want to go to Hajj this year
I really want to go
I'll pack a suitcase full of things
And learn what I should know

I'll pack some cream and simple snacks
Enough to keep me strong
I'll act the way a pilgrim acts
And won't do any wrong

I'll try my best to be my best
And come back free of sin
For when I'm there I am His guest
A righteous life begins

My Invited Home

Today I found an invite to a place,
Its name was quite familiar I confess;
Descriptions of such beauty full of grace,
It's clear that there's no sadness and distress.

I'm told I would get anything I long,
The houses made of gold - my heart inclines;
With rivers flowing never to be gone,
With fruits and drinks so pure of different kinds.

This place I'm told I'll never grow too old,
Companions there will never tell a lie;
And those who grieved on earth will be consoled,
The angels and the pure will testify.

This place I'll call my home is Paradise,
And best of all I'll get to see His Face.

True Love

My every breath is filled with Your grandeur,
I close my eyes and feel Your Majesty —
Without Your thought my life is nothing more
Than just a spec of dirt, a travesty.

I can't imagine life without Your Grace,
For many hours sitting with great pain
I yearn to be with You to see Your Face;
A time will come when I'll be there again.

But now I need to show I'm worth Your love
For all those times I turned away from You;
I know that You will always have enough,
There's nothing that I want that's not with You.

I plead with You to raise me up above
Ascending to Your garden of true love.

#52

My Secrets

This way to the exit →
Don't confuse this for Brexit!
Please return
So you can learn
The secrets of this poet

BONUS!

52 + 1

You've (kind of) reached the end of the book
But please continue to look
At all the pages
It took me ages!
To write this wonderful book.

Background to Poems

Here you'll find a brief background to some of the poems, including the meanings of a few unfamiliar words transliterated from Arabic.

The Provision (#1)

rizq = provision
bismillah = in the name of Allah

Muslims start any good action with the words "*bismillah*". The idea behind this poem is to place our trust in Allah but also make a conscious effort in gaining our worldly needs.

A Great Occasion (#2)

This is inspired by the events that took place on the 10th of Muharram. On this day, Musa (pbuh) led his people away from slavery under Pharaoh. Allah sent many signs to the leaders but they were arrogant and refused to accept Musa's call. This story can also be found in other scriptures.

Sonnet of Faith (#3)

A part of a Muslim's faith is to believe in the six components: Allah, His angels, divine revelation (books), messengers, the Day of Judgement and destiny (both the good and the bad).

A Pure Love (#4)

☘ = *sallallahu alaihi wa sallam (peace and blessings of Allah be upon him - pbuh)*
Al-Kauthar = a pond in paradise reserved for the Prophet and his followers

The love for the Prophet Muhammad supersedes a Muslim's love for any other person, and his loss is greater than the loss of any other person. That is the basis of this poem.

All by Allah's Permission (#5)

Safar used to be considered a month where bad things happened. This superstitious belief was dismissed by the Prophet (pbuh).

The Purple Sky (#7)

A reflection of the night in a city. The final third of the night is when Allah is nearest and prayers are more likely to be accepted.

A Gentle Whistle (#8)

The name is derived from the literal meaning of Safar. It delves into the thoughts of the sinner and concludes that no regular human is free of sin.

Return to Life (#9)

Rabi' = spring
Al-Awwal = the first

As the name of the month means the first spring, this poem highlights a few activities that occur at this time.

Assalaamu 'alaikum Dad (#13)
Assalaamu 'alaikum = peace be upon you

A poem originally written by my son, Haneef. As with many children that age - and perhaps most of us when we are about to embark on anything new - there is a feeling of anxiety when going to a new school.

Meant to Be (#14)
A simple structure highlighting a complex phenomenon. The whole of creation accepts the decree of the Creator, but human beings are proud and at times arrogant to acknowledge their place in the universe.

Breakdown in Communication (#16)
If no common ground is found, there is seldom any progress in relations. This poem highlights this using the voice of animals that are commonly found in the city.

The Poem that Explains the Main Reason... (#18)
Islamic culture is rich in information. There have been many books written about the message and intricate details of Islam as a way of life. This is a simple phrase that encapsulates the Prophet's role, as explained by Allah in the Quran (*surah/chapter 21:107*).

Dear Son (#22)
salah = prayer

This poem was inspired by the conversation that Luqman had with his son, which is mentioned in the Quran (*surah 31: 12-19*).

Eating Flesh (#23)

This is an all too common topic of conversation when individuals talk about others behind their backs - known as backbiting. This is a major sin in Islam and how subtly it is done is highlighted in this poem.

Our Friends (#24)

This is based on a saying of the Prophet Muhammad (pbuh). A person is upon the way of their friend(s).

The Night Journey (#26)

al-ameen = the trustworthy
buraq = the creature used to transport the Prophet
Aqsa = the third sacred mosque in Islam located in Jerusalem
miraj = ascension (into the heavens)
al-'abd = the servent

The first poem of Rajab highlights its sanctity. This is also the month where the Prophet (pbuh) was taken on a journey (*Quran, surah 17*). It is held dearly within the hearts of Muslims as this is when the five daily prayers were gifted to him.

Nearly There (#29)

The month of Sha'ban was when the Prophet (pbuh) would give freely in charity and would fast most in than any other month, except Ramadan. This poem aims to capture the importance of this month and its closeness to Ramadan. Many loved ones fail to reach the blessed month that follows.

Averter of Calamity (#30)

The importance of giving in charity is emphasised. The Prophet (pbuh) stated that giving in charity aids in pushing away calamities.

Shopping List (#31)
hasanat = rewards for good deeds
mushaf = the printed copy of the Quran

This highlights some of the important items that a Muslim requires in time for Ramadan.

I See You (#32)
From the perspective of a reflection in the mirror describing what seems to be physical defects but also the inner thoughts of someone feeling dejected in life.

The Beloved Guest (#33)
nafs = self, ego

The first poem for Ramadan expressing the deep love and affection Muslims have for this blessed month.

27ᵗʰ Night: A Sonnet for the Lonely (#36)
masjid = mosque, place of worship

Ramadan is viewed as a month where one can recharge spiritually. However, this may be a great challenge for those who have come into the faith recently and lack the supportive network. It is a reminder for them and everyone else that turning to Allah will give us the much needed serenity we all desire.

29ᵗʰ Night: Fortunate Ones (#38)
Rahman = Most gracious, entirely merciful
Raheem = especially merciful

This is dedicated to the final odd night of Ramadan. The odd nights are when the special night of decree is said to be, which is better than a thousand months (*Quran, surah 97*).

30ᵗʰ Night: The Last Slice (#39)

Just as we all try our best to make the final piece of cake or our favourite food last longer, we do the same regarding the final night. Muslims exert more energy knowing this could be their last, as no one is guaranteed to reach the next Ramadan.

Eid Poem (#40)

takbeer = saying 'Allahu akbar'
Alhamdulillah = all praise is for Allah (thank you Allah)

This was written by my son, Dawood. He has adopted the acrostic style, which is fitting as the first of Shawwal is a day of celebration, *Eid Al-Fitr*.

I'm Good Enough (#41)

This was written at a time where racial discrimination showed its ugly head. Many people around the world felt the oppression and aggression shown by those in positions of power and privilege. The poem highlights the inequalities faced by minorities on a regular basis.

The One (#43)

This poem was inspired by the short surah (chapter) in the Quran, *Al-Ikhlas (112)*. The description of Allah is so robust that only the true Creator can match it. It is very powerful and a constant reminder of the nature of our Lord.

The Call (#44)

The Islamic call to prayer can be heard in all parts of the world now. This is a tribute to it with the main body having a similar structure to the original Arabic.

Dad, Sam and Jack the Donkey (#45)
We all try to please others in our lives. This story is a reminder that we can't, and perhaps shouldn't, please everyone. The original story is well known in different cultures.

The Magpie (#46)
This was inspired by an actual magpie that I found in my garden. The most amazing part was that her parents would be around all day, and whenever I went close to her they would make a sound from afar warning me not to hurt their child. This, I felt, represented greatly a parent's love for their child.

A Flashback (#48)
The final month of the Islamic calendar is when Muslims, who are able, go on the pilgrimage. This poem touches upon my feelings on the days of Hajj. We all experience different feelings, but the most important thing is to return with our actions accepted by Allah. An accepted Hajj wipes away all of a person's past sins.

My Invited Home (#50)
This poem focuses on various aspects of Paradise, as described in Islamic texts. Every Muslim wants to achieve the highest place in Paradise, but the ultimate reward will be to see the One who created us.

True Love (#51)
The penultimate poem is about the love one feels towards Allah and His love for us, His creation. Often, in western literature and discourse, the love of Allah is omitted and His wrath is highlighted. This poem focuses on the love of Allah - a true love.

Templates & Prompts

It's time for you to write your own poems. The next few pages will provide you with the basic information on different types of poetry, insight into rhythm, and some prompts and templates for each style of poetry that you have read in this book.

Rhyme

Many poems rhyme at the end of each line or specific lines. You don't always have to do this, but the different styles of poetry I have chosen for this book mostly have rhyming patterns which are denoted with a matching letter for each rhyming line below:

Line 1	(a)
Line 2	(b)
Line 3	(a)
Line 4	(b)

Here, line 1 rhymes with line 3 and line 2 rhymes with line 4. Each type of poem will have its own rhyming pattern. These will be given to you at the start of each template as a guideline.

Syllables & Rhythm

Whether you decide to write a poem that rhymes or not, one thing to remember is that most poems follow a specific rhythm. This is usually expressed in syllables and is measured by feet and metres.

Metre = a measurement that is based on the structural pattern of a verse/poem. It is broken up into feet.

Foot = a basic unit of measurement of a metre which follows a specific pattern of stressed and unstressed syllables.

The poems in this book primarily follow the *iambic* foot. This has one unstressed *(u)* syllable followed by a stressed *(/)* syllable. See the examples below of individual words that follow the iambic pattern of stressed and unstressed syllables:

u /	*u /*	*u /*
release	detest	become

However, you can also use the iambic foot over a whole line:

u / u / u / u / u /
The scriptures sent to guide humanity

This was Shakespeare's preferred rhythm used for many of his famous poems.

Types of Poems

You would have noticed that there are different types of poems in this book. Before you start writing, the following information on each type of poem may be useful to note.

Haiku - a traditional Japanese poem made up of three lines only. It doesn't have to rhyme but traditional haiku poems have five syllables in the first and third lines, and seven syllables in the second line (5-7-5).

Limerick - a humorous poem consisting of five lines. The first, second and fifth lines must have the same rhythm and rhyme. The third and fourth lines must rhyme with each other.

Acrostic - the first letter of each line spells out a word or phrase. This type of poem doesn't have to rhyme.

Sonnet - consists of fourteen lines and is traditionally written in iambic pentameter (five sets of iambic feet). The Shakespearean sonnet follows an alternating rhyming pattern (*abab/cdcd/efef/gg*).

Ballad - is typically arranged in quatrains (four lines) with the rhyming scheme of *abab* or *abcb*. The first and third lines have four beats (iambic tetrameter), while the second and fourth lines have three beats (trimeter).

Free verse - no regular metre or rhythm. This type of poem does not necessarily follow a rhyming scheme.

Use the following pages to write your own poems in each different style.

Haiku

Have a look at poems #11, #19 and #20.

Think of a specific moment that got your attention. This could be something you saw in nature or a general observation. Note down your initial thoughts below.

_____

_____

_____

Now, simplify your thoughts and try to fit them in the 5-7-5 structure of a haiku poem.

_____

_____

_____

Limerick

Have a look at poems #12 and #42.

You can be as silly as you like with this poem. Is there anything that makes you laugh so much that you fall off your seat? What about a topic that is particular to the month that you're in now? Try including the verbs *sat* and *fly* in your first limerick.

_____(a)

_____(a)

_____(b)

_____(b)

_____(a)

Try writing another one.

_____(a)

_____(a)

_____(b)

_____(b)

_____(a)

Acrostic

Have a look at poem #40.

You may want to write a poem about something or someone you hold dear to you. Why not try writing an acrostic poem with the word 'mother'?

M_____

O_____

T_____

H_____

E_____

R_____

What about a short one?

D_____

A_____

D_____

Acrostic

Now, try writing one with your own word or phrase. Use a word that has special meaning to you and try to express that feeling through each line.

_____

_____

_____

_____

_____

_____

_____

_____

_____

_____

_____

_____

_____

Shakespearean Sonnet

Write a sonnet about something that's close to your heart. There's usually a turn in the tale around line 12, so you may want to begin with one emotion and end with another.

_____ (a)

_____ (b)

_____ (a)

_____ (b)

_____ (c)

_____ (d)

_____ (c)

_____ (d)

_____ (e)

_____ (f)

_____ (e)

_____ (f)

_____ (g)

_____ (g)

Petrarchan Sonnet

Write a sonnet about something you once loved but then lost. I've written about Ramadan in poem #33. You can choose the same topic, or another one and add human characteristics to it.

_____(a)

_____(b)

_____(b)

_____(a)

_____(a)

_____(b)

_____(b)

_____(a)

_____(c)

_____(d)

_____(c)

_____(d)

_____(c)

_____(d)

Ballad

Have a look at poems #1, #4 and #7.

Tell a short story in the form of a ballad. Write about an event that happened to you recently. What experiences and emotions did you go through during the virus outbreak?

The rhyming scheme repeats itself, but each section (stanza) may have different rhyming sets to the previous one.

_____(a)

_____(b)

_____(c)

_____(b)

_____( )

_____( )

_____( )

_____( )

_____( )

_____( )

_____( )

_____( )

Ballad

You may want to continue your first ballad here or write a new one.

_____(a)

_____(b)

_____(c)

_____(b)

_____(_)

_____(_)

_____(_)

_____(_)

_____(_)

_____(_)

_____(_)

_____(_)

Free Verse

Use this space to write about a topic that you feel very passionate about. Think about imagery and the use of similies.

_____

_____

_____

_____

_____

_____

_____

_____

_____

_____

_____

_____

_____

_____

Thank you for supporting us.

When you've finished writing your poems, why not share them with us and inspire others to start getting creative?

You can send your poems via email to
mail@giftedmuslim.com
or post online with hashtag *#giftedmuslimpoems*
and tag us *@gifted_muslim*

GIFTED MUSLIM

Made in the USA
Monee, IL
31 July 2021